Edward de Bono

JONATHAN CAPE
THIRTY BEDFORD SQUARE LONDON

FIRST PUBLISHED 1972

JONATHAN CAPE LTD, 30 BEDFORD SQUARE, LONDON WC1

ISBN 0 224 00723 8

PRINTED AND BOUND BY
EBENEZER BAYLIS AND SON LTD
THE TRINITY PRESS, WORCESTER AND LONDON

Introduction

The purpose of this short booklet is to outline what I am about. I am interested in 'thinking' because the traditional philosophic approach seems to have resulted only in abstract and complicated word-games which have not been of much practical use. Yet thinking as a practical process is a fascinating subject; for it is rather an important part of everyone's life.

For instance there is about 'creativity' an aura of mystique. I invented the neutral term 'lateral thinking' so as to be able to deal with the type of thinking that was involved in generating new ideas and escaping from old ones. In contrast to traditional vertical thinking, which takes place after you have accepted fixed ideas, lateral thinking is a sideways movement in search of new ideas. Lateral thinking is an attempt to make creativity tangible and understandable in terms of the basic processes involved. The 'idea ingredient' in thinking is becoming more important all the time.

But creativity is only one part of thinking and I am just as interested in the other parts. My book, *Practical Thinking*, is about the different ways of being right and the different ways of being wrong; and the tricks, devices and habits used in everyday thinking.

There are many ideas which I have not written down, or published, or talked about. But this booklet is intended to give some sort of order and perspective to books that are already available, by showing how each book is independent yet forms part of the whole picture.

The Myth of the Monohops

Monohop society was intensely logical. Early in the development of this culture, the sociologists had come to the conclusion that most of society's troubles arose directly from man's ability to attack his fellows and from his ability to run away. The former encouraged aggression, the latter crime. It was agreed that if man's mobility could be reduced at an early enough age society would benefit. Therefore soon after birth the left leg was amputated from each monohop child.

With its usual rapid adaptation, society soon organized itself into a monohop world. Bicycles had but one pedal, right shoes were the only shoes ever made, all staircases were abolished and replaced by lifts and escalators. In short, so completely did society become monohop that no one noticed any inconvenience.

Whenever anyone suggested that a two-legged society might be preferable, he was met not by hostility but by puzzlement. Why, They asked, should we change? Everything is running smoothly. Wouldn't we have to go to great expense to make and buy left shoes? Wouldn't our bicycles be useless? And what about unemployment among surgeons and lift-makers? What about aggression and crime – we know there would be a great increase? Besides, can you *prove* that change would be better, have you collected statistical evidence to show that two-legged monohops would be better than the usual variety? But, said the revolutionary, is it not obvious that a man with two legs can do all that a man with one leg can do – and more as well? That may well be, They said, but monohops are clearly best suited to this monohop world. We are concerned only with getting our people to hop as excellently as possible (we have exams, you know), not with how much better life would be if we had two legs instead of one.

Old Think

It has been suggested that the three greatest intellectual disasters in Western culture were the ancient Greeks, the Crucifixion and the

Renaissance. I do see the point of this suggestion, but I would draw a sharp distinction between the extremism, the polarization and the right/wrong certainty of the Crucifixion, and Christianity as such which innovated exactly opposing attitudes.

The traditional idiom of thinking, started by the Greek philosophers and nurtured by the Renaissance, suggests that somehow, somewhere, an absolute truth is set high on a mountain and that with sufficient intelligence and education anyone can mount the carefully polished concept steps that lead there. This attitude is nicely illustrated by Bertrand Russell in his Nobel Prize lecture: ' ... the main thing needed to make the world happy is intelligence. And this is after all an optimistic conclusion, because intelligence is a thing that can be fostered by known methods of education.' Is this so? Nearly all the conflict situations in history have been brought about by the better-educated people on each side. What Bertrand Russell might have meant was that everyone who agreed with the enlightened way he, Bertrand Russell, thought was intelligent and well educated. That is the traditional use of the word 'intelligent'. Or he may have meant that there was some high level of intelligence which, once achieved, would result in everyone coming to the same conclusions. If so, then we have no right to assume that known methods of education will enable us ever to reach an intelligence that has been so obviously unattainable in the past.

In practice it seems that people start out with a different way of looking at things and then use their intelligence and education to support *that point of view*. Since the old idiom of thinking insists that there is an absolutely *right* way to look at things, then anybody who reaches a way that seems right to him necessarily feels that any opposing point of view must be wrong (and hence need altering). It is certainly not a lack of intelligence or education that allows people to think in different ways – simply the fact that they are living in different worlds furnished by different experience, perceptions and emotions.

The more one looks into thinking the more one comes to realize that:

1. Everyone is always right

2. No one is ever right

In other words, within your own perceptual world you are always right, but this is not everyone else's world and certainly not an absolute one. Once you accept this idea, then the emphasis shifts away from proving the logical rightness of your own point of view and the logical wrongness of the other person's point of view on the assumption that you are both looking at the same thing.

There is a story of a man who painted half his car white and the other half black. He said he did this because he loved to hear the witnesses dogmatically contradict each other whenever he was involved in an accident. A wife tries on a new dress and loves it. Her husband who is with her dislikes it. She is looking at the colour and shape – he is looking at the price.

The emphasis shifts from proving the other person wrong to exploring what he is really looking at. And if he does seem to have an inadequate point of view then one tries to bring about a change in this, not by forceful dogmatism but by developing the type of thinking which will allow him to switch over and look at things in a different way. Unfortunately the traditional idiom of thinking is not good at doing this because it insists that logical rightness is absolute. One needs a new idiom of thinking that is based not on dogmatic proof but on the creative ability to change ideas. It is this sort of change that leads to a different way of looking at things, and the switch-over to that new way is insight.

An Englishman may learn to speak German very fluently. He may get more and more skilled all the time. But he will never reach a point at which his excellence in German is such that he suddenly finds himself speaking Italian. No amount of excellence in the old idiom of thinking will enable you suddenly to switch over to a new idiom. If you happen to be in Italy, then a few words mumbled in Italian are worth more than any degree of excellence in German.

To criticize the old idiom of thinking does not mean that it is wrong, but just sometimes inappropriate. Furthermore it is not necessary to have developed the new idiom to the same pitch of excellence as the old one before it can be useful. Someone using the new idiom is not necessarily more skilled in thinking than someone using the old idiom – a person mumbling a few words in Italian could not claim to be a better linguist than the person who is fluent in German, but the person who is fluent in both could make this claim.

Computers and Thinking

Some years ago I was using computers to work out some complicated mathematics in the course of my medical research. Like everyone else, I was much impressed by the superb efficiency of the machines which seemed on the point of making human thinking superfluous. Reacting against this, I became interested in that type of thinking in which the human mind still surpassed computers. This was the type of thinking required for creativity and invention: the generation of new ideas and the escape from old ones.

It seemed likely that in the future, as computers took over the 'processing' part of thinking, the 'idea' part would become more and more important. On the whole, computers are so uncreative that in order for them to work at all you have to give them the starting 'ideas' and the instructions for dealing with them. The computer then processes the ideas according to the instructions and gives you the result that arises from the combination of those ideas and those instructions. Suppose you wanted a computer to tell you how Shakespeare's Othello should have behaved. You might start by giving definite values to such things as loss of life, disappointment, trustworthiness of Iago, usefulness of a dead Desdemona, etc. Then you would instruct the computer to use a mathematical technique (perhaps the well-known Games Theory) to work out the best course of action for Othello. The computer would end up by telling you that Othello's best course of action was to strangle Desdemona and that (since she was to be strangled anyway) Desdemona might just as well have deceived him. This apparently odd answer would be no fault of the computer or of Games Theory. The answer is determined by how the situation is looked at in the first place: whether it is seen as a conflict situation; what factors are taken into consideration; the importance or values that are given to the chosen factors, and so on. It is this initial 'idea' stage (or perceptual stage) that really determines the answer. The 'processing' stage, however excellent, can do no more than tell you what is implicit in the idea stage. Thus the two stages of thinking are:

1. The idea stage

2. The processing stage

In fact the very excellence of the computer in the processing stage places a growing burden on the human mind, which has to set up the starting ideas. Not only does the human mind have to set up questions for the computer to answer but also it has to make sense of the answers.

We are told we live in a world of exploding *information*; every day there is more and more to learn. But actually we live in a world of exploding *data* – not information. Ideas are the spectacles through which we have to look at data in order to see information. We act on information, not on data. And, contrary to what most scientists are taught, data cannot turn into information without ideas. It is as necessary to learn how to generate ideas as it is to learn how to generate and process data.

It is in this first stage of thinking (the pre-logical idea stage) that the creativity of the human mind cannot yet be replaced by computers. When it is replaced, then the computers will decide on the world that is best for computers to live in – with humans as their mates.

First-stage Thinking and Second-stage Thinking

At the end of the first stage of thinking we have a *way of looking at things*. We have parcelled up the situation into concepts, factors, values, relationships, etc. We then hand over this concept package to the logical processing of the second stage of thinking. The logical processing sets to work and gives us the right answer for that particular starting package. Unfortunately the excellent logical processing of the second stage cannot be used in the first stage because it can only go to work on a definite package.

In the traditional thinking idiom the first stage of thinking is ignored for two reasons. First it is assumed that the traditional bundle of fixed concepts is the right and only proper way to look at things. Second it is assumed that no matter with what 'concept package' you start you will still get the right answer if your logical processing is good enough. Unfortunately both these assumptions are limiting and even dangerous. You cannot ignore the first stage of thinking unless you believe in the unique and absolute validity of your way of looking at things and have the force to impose this view on others (and so create a self-justifying world as we have always tried to do).

Since the logical processing that we use in the second stage cannot be applied in the first stage of thinking, we have to develop a different type of thinking for generating new ideas and escaping from old ones. This is the creative type of thinking which I call *lateral thinking* since it involves moving sideways from one way of looking at things to another.

My first book, *The Use of Lateral Thinking*, was written to show the difference between lateral thinking and the logical sequential thinking of the old idiom (vertical thinking). Vertical thinking is like digging the same hole deeper; lateral thinking is moving sideways to dig a new hole in a different place. Vertical thinking takes place after you have accepted fixed concepts; lateral thinking before you have found new ones.

Since lateral thinking is neither logical nor sequential it seems to work in exactly the opposite way to computers. The paradox is that computer people more than anyone else see the absolute necessity for lateral thinking. This is because they are more aware than any traditional thinker of the huge importance of the first stage of thinking. As suggested above, classical logicians feel that, no matter where they start, if their logic is good enough they will come to the right answer. Computer people know that this is nonsense. The answer you reach is only consistent with the starting assumptions you have made. Furthermore if you look at the situation in certain ways you may be unable to get any answer at all. Even if you do eventually reach an answer, a poor choice of concept package may mean that you use twenty-five times as much expensive computer time as you would with a more creative package.

Lateral Thinking

I often get asked why it was necessary to invent the term 'lateral thinking' if all I mean is creativity. It is suggested that the invention of the term is simply a way of attracting attention, like relabelling an old bottle. There is of course a real value in relabelling an old bottle if it serves to bring back into attention something that has been ignored or taken for granted. But in fact there are two very definite reasons for inventing the neutral term 'lateral thinking'.

'Creativity' is a wide term and a vague one. Above all, it is the description of a *result*. When something has come about which is both effective and original, we then say that creative thinking must have been involved. But a creative *result* can come about in very different ways: chance, special experience, the coming together of ideas that are usually separate, dreams, delirium, drugs, mistakes, bloody-mindedness, etc. There are some research projects in progress whose aim is to explain creativity by examining in detail what went on before the creative result. I think this hindsight approach is rather futile, since the label 'creative' may be attached to the result of a procedure that would lead to failure on every other occasion.

Whereas 'creativity' is the description of a result, lateral thinking is a *process*. A result can only be admired, but a process can be learned and used. If you are successful in using lateral thinking then the result you come up with will be creative. At other times you may use lateral thinking and not come up with a result at all – but you are still using the process. The process is of course only useful if you come up with results often enough. Lateral thinking is not, however, one particular technique or gimmick. It is a way of thinking with its own basic principles, just as logical thinking is a way of thinking with its own basic principles.

Since creativity has been neglected in most other fields, there is about it a strong flavour of artistic achievement. Until recently creativity has been a matter of literature, music, painting, etc. Such artistic 'creativity' involves a talent for expression, aesthetic values, craftsmanship, style, emotional resonance, ego-mania, and so on, all of which are distinct from the ability to generate new ideas and escape from old ones – which is what constitutes lateral thinking.

Finally creativity has about it the aura of a semi-mystical gift which one either has or envies. Lateral thinking is much more simply a way of thinking, a way of using ideas and information. It is because we have never bothered to develop this way of thinking that we have to rely on all the other haphazard processes that go to make up creativity.

I am often asked by educationists whether lateral thinking is the same as divergent thinking. Divergent thinking is *part* of lateral thinking in so far as it is one of the ways of escaping from obvious ideas in order to find new ones. But lateral thinking is concerned not only with opening up a plethora of possibilities but with bringing about an effective restructuring of the situation. The divergent aspect of lateral thinking is only one among many other aspects.

'Insight thinking' would be the nearest equivalent to lateral thinking, for here one switches from the usual way of looking at something to a new way that is more effective. But 'insight' and 'intuition', like 'creativity', are only descriptions of results.

The interesting thing is that though lateral thinking is based directly on consideration of the mind as a patterning system, the conclusions seem to agree well with the experience of those who have a more empirical approach.

The Nature of Lateral Thinking

In *The Use of Lateral Thinking* the nature of lateral thinking is shown by contrasting it with traditional vertical thinking, and by giving various examples of its use. Further examples are given below:

1. An ambulance hurrying along a narrow country lane comes up behind a flock of sheep which completely fills the lane. There is no way of driving the sheep off the road. How does the ambulance get past the sheep?

2. The lane beside my cottage is a blind alley, so that new visitors who drive down the lane always request my assistance when it comes to getting out, since there is not enough space to turn a car round and there are no street lights. How else could they manage?

3. The designers of a skyscraper had not been told that it was to be used as an office block, so there were too few lifts for the number of people who wanted to use them. As a result the staff became dissatisfied and started to leave. What could be done?

These problems are trivial in themselves. They are used as illustrations because they require no special background information and the solution is obvious once it has been found. They are used to illustrate the *process* of the lateral move away from the obvious approach to a new one.

Answers:

1. In the ambulance problem the straightforward approach is to try and get the ambulance past the sheep, for instance by stringing out the sheep along the side of the road so that the ambulance can get past. At worst the ambulance could drive forward slowly enough for the sheep to get out of its way. The lateral move is to stop trying to get the ambulance past the sheep and instead try to get the sheep past the ambulance. So it is the ambulance that stops and then the flock is turned round and the sheep filter back past the stationary ambulance.

2. Only one in ten drivers think of using their direction indicators

to illuminate the road behind them with intermittent flashes. This is because you have to move laterally from considering them only as indicators to considering them as lights (brake lights will also do, but are less satisfactory).

3. The architects and engineers, when consulted, decided that there were two possible approaches: put in more lifts or increase the use of existing lifts (by speeding them up, staggering working hours, etc.). Someone else, however, made a lateral move and came up with a solution that was very much easier and cheaper. Instead of considering the lifts, he moved sideways to consider the impatience of the staff. This was so effectively reduced, by placing mirrors around the entrances to the lifts, that there were no further complaints.

The above three problems are almost too simple to solve. Once you have made the lateral move for yourself (or read the answer) it all seems obvious. Furthermore once you have seen the answer it all seems very logical. It is a fundamental characteristic of lateral thinking that the solutions it produces always seem obvious and logical in hindsight even though they may have been anything but obvious in foresight (for example, only one in ten drivers used their indicators). The reason for this is that the human mind works as a patterning system (as discussed later), and in a patterning system the route from A to B is not the same as the route from B to A. It is precisely this difficulty in reaching a solution that should have been obvious that makes lateral thinking so essential – and humour possible.

Two more difficult problems that require lateral thinking for their solution are given below:

4. There are 111 entrants for the Wimbledon singles tennis tournament. As an umpire you have to try and arrange the minimum number of matches that have to be played. How would you set about finding this minimum number?

5. A glass of oil and a glass of vinegar stand side by side. You take a spoonful of oil and stir it into the vinegar. You then take a spoonful

from the vinegar glass and put it back into the oil glass. At this point is there more oil in the vinegar or vinegar in the oil glass?

Whenever I give the tennis tournament problem in the course of my lectures, everyone reaches for a pencil and paper. This happens even if the audience is made up of sophisticated problem-solvers. Yet by making a lateral move the problem can be solved in five seconds without any working-out at all. Instead of working through to see how many matches would be required to produce a winner, you make a lateral move and see how many matches are required to produce the losers. Since there is but one winner there must be 110 losers, and since each match produces only one loser (who cannot play again) there must be 110 matches. I included this problem once in an article I did for the IBM journal and to my surprise I got several furious letters from rigid-thinking readers to say that it just could not be so.

The oil/vinegar problem is an old one but an extraordinary one. When I used a version of it in *The Use of Lateral Thinking* I got many dogmatic letters saying that I must have made a mistake. One such letter came from a university lecturer who was actually giving a course on 'thinking'. This particular person was very quick to see his mistake, but others have remained convinced that the answer given in the book must be wrong. In a recent lecture to a university audience (presumably among the best-educated 5 per cent of the population) only six out of two hundred reached the right answer.

It is not the fact that people make mistakes or have difficulty in reaching the right answer which makes the problem fascinating to me (I probably make such mistakes more often than they do); the fascinating part is how people are *completely convinced of the rightness of a demonstrably wrong answer*. It was this that also fascinated a judge who had read the book and then tried the problem on his colleagues. The point is that people who refuse to make a lateral move and change their approach can so easily be convinced of the absolute rightness of what is demonstrably wrong. 'Neutral' logic actually generates a great deal of fierce emotion. The implications of this problem for real-life situations are of course profound and rather frightening. The danger of this arrogance of logic is discussed in another book, *Practical Thinking*, to be considered later.

The usual answer for the oil/vinegar problem is that since a spoonful of *pure* oil is exchanged for a spoonful of *mixture*, there must be more oil in the vinegar glass than vinegar in the oil glass. Though this seems very simple and logical it is unfortunately quite wrong. Nor is it necessary to use mathematics to reach the right answer. The reader is left to make the lateral move for himself.

Why Lateral Thinking is Necessary

If you hand different-shaped wooden blocks one by one to a child and ask him to build a tower, he will simply add each new block to the existing structure. The tower that results is not nearly so stable as the one he would have built had he been given all the blocks at the same time. In the first case the structure of the tower would be determined by the sequence in which the child received the blocks. In the second case he would be free to make the best use of all the available blocks.

Whenever information arrives piece by piece, the way it gets put together is determined by the particular sequence of arrival. Hence the final arrangement of information is very unlikely to make the best use of what is available. This 'best use' would be the arrangement arrived at if all the information had been available at once instead of arriving piece by piece. Unfortunately, with personal experience, social history, cultural history, the growth of ideas and the growth of institutions or organizations, the information arrives piece by piece and gets arranged according to this sequence of arrival. The result is that, like the child with the blocks, one is trapped by the particular sequence of arrival.

The human mind, being a patterning system, is particularly susceptible to such sequence effects. It works by setting up ideas and then extending them by addition rather than restructuring them to make a better use of already available information.

In my lectures I use a simple way of showing how easy it is to be trapped by the sequence effect. I hand a series of small flat plastic pieces to someone, with instructions to arrange them in the simplest way possible. The pieces are not given all at once but in a sequence. The result is shown in the diagram below. The first two pieces are quickly arranged to form a rectangle. The square piece which arrives next is simply added to the existing rectangle to give a longer rectangle. But when the next two pieces arrive, there is great difficulty in finding a simple arrangement for all the pieces.

I have carried out this experiment about two hundred times in the course of lectures and on other occasions, and only twice has a person been able to escape from the sequence in which the pieces are presented (it is of course much more difficult to do this when you

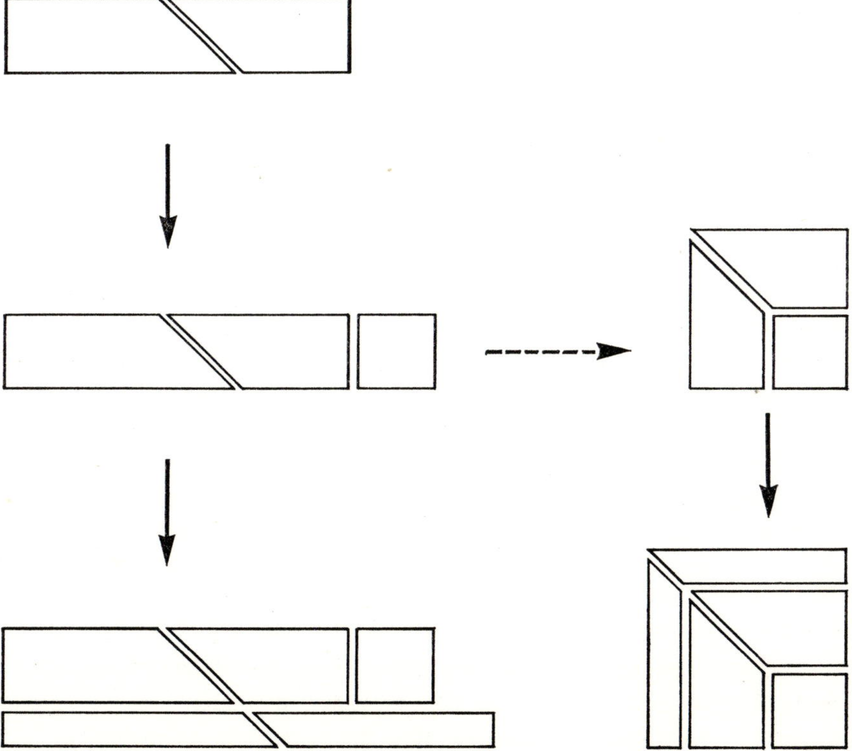

know everyone is watching you). In order to escape from the sequence trap, you have to go back and restructure what was a *perfectly adequate arrangement* at the time. You have to make a lateral move and restructure the long rectangle as a square. The next move is then absurdly easy (whereas before it seemed impossible). The process is shown on page 17.

Lateral thinking is necessary in order to escape from the sequence of experience that makes us look at things in a particular way. For instance, one has only to consider the rise of industrial society, capital exploitation of labour, the early days of trade unionism, the great depression, etc., to see how present-day industrial attitudes depend on historical sequence rather than on the best use of available knowledge. The same sequence effect can be seen in our attitudes to crime. Here the sequence of ideas has moved from crime as a sin (involving responsibility, guilt, punishment, purification, etc.) to crime as a psychological aberration or reaction to social deprivation. The result is confusion. For instance, most people would feel much less horrified by the idea of capital punishment than by the idea of using surgical or chemical treatment to make a criminal fit in better with the requirements of society. Such interference would be considered barbaric and inhuman, whereas capital punishment is (almost) civilized.

You can sometimes see a very neat example of the sequence effect if you watch someone dealing with a kebab in a restaurant. It is obvious that the chunks of meat have been placed on the skewer one by one, so the diner holds the skewer firmly and tries to force the meat off with his fork. As a result it scatters all over the table. The best thing is to forget how the meat got on to the skewer, and to make a lateral move by trying to get the skewer away from the meat rather than the meat away from the skewer. So you hold the meat steady with a fork and simply *withdraw* the skewer. This example is extremely trivial, but it is significant for two reasons. First, because we make a great fuss of historical development and often forget how easy it is to be trapped by it. Second, because even in our mathematical systems we depend largely on the assumption that the best route from A to B is also the best route from B to A – and this just is not so in patterning systems like the brain.

Therefore the need for lateral thinking arises directly from the need to escape from the obvious way of looking at things inevitably set up by the sequence effect of experience. Only if we develop this ability can we hope to make better use of already available knowledge.

Method and Techniques

Appreciating the results of lateral thinking, or understanding the need for lateral thinking, is not the same as deliberately setting out to achieve such results. Lateral thinking is a way of thinking, with certain fundamental principles. For practical purposes the principles can be incorporated in various specific techniques which can be learned and used. Nevertheless these techniques are only a way of applying the principles of lateral thinking, just as the syllogism is only a way of applying logic.

The practical use of lateral thinking can be considered under the following headings:

1. Removing the 'uncreativity' fostered by the traditional thinking idiom implicit in our education.

2. Understanding the fundamental principles of lateral thinking (which relate directly to the way the mind works as a patterning system).

3. Learning and practising specific techniques for putting the principles into use.

4. Becoming familiar with the new operational word PO which is as fundamental to lateral thinking as NO is to logical thinking.

The practical use of lateral thinking is set out in two books, each of which is written for a specific purpose. *Lateral Thinking: A Textbook of Creativity* is intended to provide a practical basis for the teaching of lateral thinking in schools and throughout education, the idea being that the subject should be taught for one hour every week. *Lateral Thinking For Management* is intended to provide a basis for the understanding, training, organization and use of creativity in business, and it suggests practical techniques for this purpose.

It is suggested that before reading either of the above books, you should read *The Use of Lateral Thinking*, which provides a general introduction to the subject. Such an introduction is necessary in order to put the various practical techniques into their proper perspective.

Misconceptions

One

There are those who feel that since the principles of lateral thinking are quite contrary to the principles of logical thinking, I must be against logic. Nothing could be further from the truth. I appreciate as much as anyone else the immense usefulness and effectiveness of logical thinking. The two aspects of logic which I am against have nothing to do with the basic process itself but only with the way it is used and the attitudes that are sometimes attached to it. These two aspects are:

1. The arrogance and righteousness of logic, which assumes that a conclusion correctly derived from certain starting assumptions has an absolute validity outside these assumptions.

2. The ineffectiveness of logic in bringing about creative changes.

Together these aspects indicate the 'incompleteness' of logic. I do believe that logic is excellent in the second or processing stage of thinking but of no use in the first or idea stage.

Lateral thinking is no more anti-logic than an orange is anti-apple. They are simply different. Both are necessary. Each is of use at a particular stage of thinking. If the forward gears of a car are provided by logic, mathematics, etc., then the reverse gear is provided by lateral thinking. You would not dream of driving in reverse gear all day long. But unless you have the ability to use the reverse gear you are certain to be trapped by the first blind alley you come to.

Two

Since the results it achieves are always logical in *hindsight*, there are those who feel that lateral thinking is no more than a plea for better logic. This shows a complete lack of understanding of the nature of a patterning system. It is very easy to devise problems that are difficult to solve whose solutions, in hindsight, are so obvious that the difficulty cannot have been simply one of logic.

The principles of lateral thinking are fundamentally different from the principles of logical thinking. The most basic principle of all in logic is that *you must be right at each stage*; without this principle, logic would cease to exist. Yet in lateral thinking it is not enough to be right at each stage – in fact one may even be quite deliberately wrong. Logical thinking is also based on continuity, since one moves smoothly along a logical sequence. Lateral thinking seeks to break continuity; in fact PO, a new operant word for the use of lateral thinking, may be regarded as a device to introduce discontinuity. There are several other fundamental points of difference.

It is of course perfectly logical to learn and use lateral thinking – otherwise I should not be writing about it. Once one appreciates the need to escape from old ideas and to generate new ones then it becomes very logical to set about using processes that are not themselves logical at all. Yet even these illogical processes are logically derived from the nature of a patterning system.

The Use of New Ideas

There are four main areas for the use of creativity and new ideas:

1. Innovation
2. Problem-solving
3. Simplification
4. Alternatives

Most people only think of the first one and suppose that they can do without creativity, since they are not designers, inventors or artists.

Innovation
This is an obvious use of creativity. It is a matter of new inventions, new designs, new styles, new theories; in fact, new ideas of any sort, which leap forward from the present state of knowledge.

Problem-solving
Few people set out to be inventors but everyone has problems. Often problems are created only by the particular way one looks at a situation. This is the way that has been determined by the sequence of experience. As soon as one can break out of this way of looking at things the problem disappears. At other times a particular approach makes a problem very difficult or even impossible to solve. Yet a change of approach makes a solution very easy (for example, in the tennis tournament problem). Even if one is using mathematical problem-solving techniques, creativity plays an important part in the way the problem is looked at before the techniques are chosen or applied.

Simplification
Ideas, like organizations, grow more complex and more cumbersome. This is because changes are simply added on. It is easy to add, difficult to subtract and almost impossible to restructure. There comes a time when creative restructuring can simplify things enormously. This cycle of complication followed by simplification is very evident in the world of design and also in science. A good example is insulin, which was at first supposed to have all sorts of complicated actions; these were then reduced to the single action of facilitating the entry of glucose into cells. The moment of simplification usually involves a new idea which breaks away from the old way of looking at things to provide a new, simpler way that may have been available for a long time.

Alternatives
One can make decisions about the past by examining all the available

data – one would not want to make decisions on incomplete data. But in planning and making decisions about the future one has no data except what can be obtained by extrapolating past data. When the rate of change is as high as it is today, this extrapolation can be very dangerous. In order to create an adequate framework for future decisions one has to generate as many alternatives as possible. This is a matter for creativity. Creativity is also involved in generating the alternative explanations offered for some event. Such alternatives are the basis of progress in science and without them one is dangerously trapped in the certainty of ignorance.

Mania for Change

It is often said that there is too much mania for change and that change creates more problems than it solves. It is certainly easy to point to technological change and the problems created by atomic energy, pollution and supersonic airliners, for example.

But it is not the technological change itself that causes the trouble, but the *unchanged ideas* that direct, control and use the technology. The atomic bomb is the result of a very very old idea: make your weapon as powerful as you possibly can. Pollution is the result of a very very old idea: throw things away and forget about them. Supersonic airliners are the result of a very very old idea: travel as fast as you possibly can. It is not a matter of stopping change but of learning to change the ideas that control technology.

The danger is not that we have too much change: it is that we have mechanisms of change in the technological world, but none in the world of thinking, because our old idiom of thinking has never developed methods for changing ideas.

The Mechanism of Mind

Over the ages philosophers, in their attempts to explain the mind, have had nothing more substantial to play with than words. These word-games have been intricate, and even beautiful, but not often helpful. The alternative to playing word-games has been to regard the mind as a medieval mystery for ever beyond explanation.

At last, however, we have made enough progress in biology and in the understanding of information systems to go beyond word-games and mysticism to look at the mind as the direct behaviour of the nerve system of the brain. We know how nerves work and we know how self-organizing systems work, so it is possible now to understand mind as the direct behaviour of one type of information system. There are those who feel that any mechanical explanation of mind destroys the beauty which the mind has when regarded as a mystery. But knowledge of the anatomy of a ballerina's legs or even of the molecular chemistry of the muscles does nothing to impair an appreciation of the over-all performance.

It is true that we cannot yet fill in all the details of the mechanism of mind, but we can say very definite things about the broad class of information systems to which it belongs. Both a horse and a motor-cycle are means of getting from one place to another. You sit astride them and steer by pulling on the front end. But you would not get very far by whipping a motor-cycle or filling a horse up with petrol. In order to use a system effectively, you need to know the broad characteristics of that system. Fine detail (for example, the cardio-respiratory physiology of a horse or the compression ratio of the motor-cycle engine) might add surprisingly little to the effectiveness with which you use the system.

As with the horse and motor-cycle, the characteristics of two types of system may be very different even though the outcome appears the same. Consider the following two types of information system:

1. *Externally organized system.* On a table there is a box containing a variety of plastic pieces of different colours and shapes. The pieces are so arranged in the box that you can find whichever sort of piece you want. You take out the pieces you need and put them together in significant arrangements.

2. *Self-organized system.* A flat dish contains ordinary table jelly

(gelatine). Spoonfuls of hot water are poured on to the surface of the jelly. While the water is hot it dissolves the gelatine so that there is a shallow depression when the fluid is poured off. Eventually the surface of the jelly becomes eroded into a system of channels much as a landscape is eroded into a system of rivers. If a spoonful is now poured on the surface at one spot, it does not stay there but moves along the channel to a different spot – just as if it had been placed in that different spot to begin with. Thus the *surface itself* is actively moving things around.

In the first type of system the material is picked out and then moved around by a separate processor. This is the type of system that operates in a computer; it is also the one that traditionally is supposed to operate in the mind.

In the second type of system the surface is neutral but is gradually altered by incoming information which eventually comes to move itself around – without the need for any outside processor. The information becomes its own processor in the environment provided by the jelly surface. Contrary to the traditional view, this seems to be the sort of system that operates in the mind.

The first half of *The Mechanism of Mind* describes the type of information system operating in the mind, by means of simple models such as the jelly model used above. The second half of the book is about the natural behaviour of this type of system and how it relates directly to the way we think. It explains why attention must be limited and unified and how this chops up the world into separate concepts. It explains the basis both of gradual learning and of instant insight-learning. It explains the physical basis of such phenomena as humour, abstraction, assimilation, polarization and other behaviour which is usually considered to be mysterious and uniquely human. It explains how, above all, the system has immense advantages but also inescapable limitations, and how these limitations affect our thinking. This book, the most fundamental of all my books, provides the basis for the others. Nevertheless the other books are written so as to make sense on their own. As suggested before, it has been interesting to see how a consideration of the system basis of mind leads to ideas that agree with the direct experience of others.

Philosophy's traditional view is that it is the excellence of the human mind that allows us to think so well. If one is playing the usual philosophy word-games then it is simply not possible to come to any other conclusion. It is only when looking at the physical basis of mind that one comes across some strange paradoxes. For instance, if you had a camera which recorded only a tiny portion of what you saw in the view-finder and distorted even that, you would be horrified by such deficiency. And yet it is precisely this sort of deficiency that makes the mind able to think at all. Another paradox is that the humour process is really more *significant* in thinking (but not more important) than the reasoning process. This is because the mind works as a patterning system, and without the humour process there would be no way of escaping from established patterns. Reason is easily imitable by machine, but it would be very sinister if computers could laugh because then they would be capable of creativity and probably 'self' as well. The ability to make mistakes is also one of the major advantages of mind from the point of view of progress.

Blocked by Openness

The most fundamental characteristic of a patterning system is the paradox of being blocked because there is nothing in the way. This process is illustrated in the diagram on page 27 in which the width of the path indicates its familiarity (as carved out by experience). If you start at the beginning you have no choice but to go shooting along the wide-open path. You do not even notice the side-turning that leads to the solution. The only way to reach the solution is to turn back and deliberately look around for alternative paths. You could try and ignore the obvious path, but in practice this is impossible just as it is impossible for the water in the jelly model to flow from a deep channel into a shallower one. The diagram also indicates how a solution is obvious in *hindsight* because it is very easy to find your way back to the starting point.

When I was at Harvard I tried out a series of very simple problems on some of the senior academic staff. There was one problem, which most people can solve in fifteen seconds, that some of the professors puzzled over for as long as ten minutes and then had to give up. The only peculiarity of the problem was that to solve it you had to reverse out of the obvious approach and find a different approach

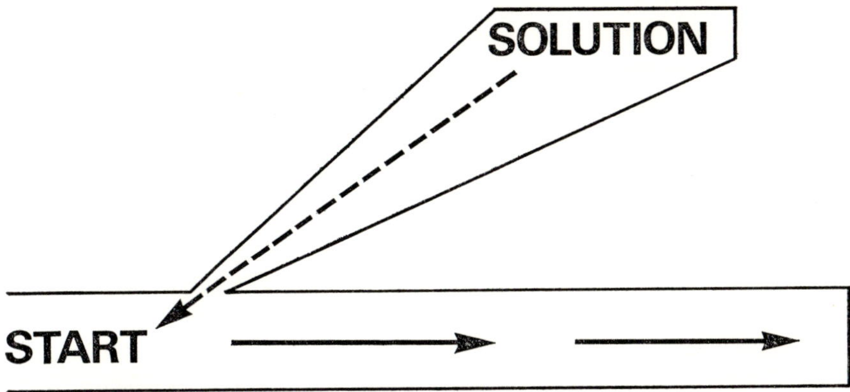

whereupon it became very easy. Those who had difficulty were blocked by openness. They felt that if they were right at each stage it must be possible to solve the problem by going forward. They could not accept that it might be necessary to go back and try a different approach. I have come across this phenomenon again and again in people who by academic standards are unusually brilliant (for example, a double first in classics at Cambridge University).

Concept graveyard

If you think of the mind as the table-top system described on page 24 (the traditional view), and concepts as the coloured pieces of plastic, then it is obvious that you can choose or ignore whichever pieces you want. The problem of being blocked by openness simply never arises. Moreover the greater the number of concepts you have the better it is since you can simply ignore those you do not want.

But if you consider the other type of system described, and think of concepts not as separate items but as road junctions in the patterning system, then the choice of one concept or pathway immediately commits you to a particular way of looking at things. The phenomenon of being blocked by openness now becomes very real and very important.

The concepts that we *do* have impede our thinking more than the concepts that we do not have. Consider the concepts of 'memory' and 'recall'. They immediately determine that one looks at the mind in terms of a memory store and a separate processor that uses the store. This makes it very difficult to regard the memory and the processor as one and the same thing – as in a self-organizing system. Other concepts which can exert a blocking effect include: agency, act, responsibility, free-will, guilt, meaning and rationality.

The trouble is that the human mind has a natural tendency to create more and more concepts by splitting up the old ones or relating them one to another. While the mind has this ability to create concepts, it has no mechanism for killing them. We badly need a concept graveyard for concepts that have outlived their usefulness. But as a patterning system the mind can never kill concepts because it works in the opposite direction – to establish patterns ever more firmly. The alternative to a concept graveyard is some means for keeping the concepts but escaping from them occasionally. Lateral thinking is a means for doing this.

The Mind in Action

Lateral thinking is only one aspect of thinking. It is important in the same way as the reverse gear is important in a car. But you do not drive in reverse gear the whole time. Much of the time in thinking, you are not trying to change ideas but instead are trying to use the ideas you have in an effective way.

What does happen in thinking? Does the mind really take those nice logical steps which it is supposed to take? Or is actual thinking much more messy, and logic no more than a way of tidying up afterwards in order to impress other people? Perhaps some people really do use logic all the time, but others reach the same results in a different way.

The Five-Day Course in Thinking was written to provide a direct opportunity for readers to watch their own thinking in action. The book consists of a series of related problem-situations which grow out of one another. None of them requires any previous knowledge or mathematical ability. Getting the right answer to the problems is not nearly so important as observing how you get the wrong answer or understanding why you cannot get any answer at all. There are really three five-day courses:

1. Insight thinking: the solution tends to come all at once or not at all. (The reader is required to balance knives on bottles, etc.)

2. Sequential thinking: the solution is arrived at stage by stage. (Involves arranging matchboxes so that they touch one another in specified ways.)

3. Strategic thinking: no specific solutions, but the development of guidelines for action. (Introduces the L-game which was designed as a very simple game that could nevertheless be played with a high degree of skill: each player has only one piece but there are more than 18,000 positions.)

In working through this book the reader has a chance to observe whether he actually plans every move in advance or whether he *plays around* and makes good use of what turns up. He might notice whether having solved a similar problem in the past helps or hinders him solve the current problem. He can also observe the difficulties of sequential thinking, in which the second step can often undo the first one. Thinking is not an abstract set of rules which you either know or do not know, but a fascinating process which you can learn about simply by watching.

Practical Thinking

The traditional approach to thinking concentrates on the way we *should* think. The aim is to develop idealized logical processes and make them ever more refined and abstract until in the end one has such perfections as Mathematical Logic. Such abstract systems are very good in themselves but have nothing to do with practical everyday thinking. The attitude is somewhat like that of a glass-blower who concentrates on producing perfect specimens and discards the flawed specimens because they should not happen.

Contrast these two approaches to thinking:

This is the idealized and perfect way you should think. This is what you should be doing. Aim towards this ideal all the time.

This is the way the mind works. These are the mistakes, habits, tricks and devices the mind uses in thinking. Be prepared to make such mistakes, etc., and learn to recognize and pick them out both in your own thinking and in the thinking of others.

I prefer the latter approach which is more practical – and rather easier. After all, the idealized abstract approach of perfection has been around for centuries and seems to have done very little for ordinary everyday thinking.

The book *Practical Thinking* is based directly on a series of experiments designed to investigate the way people think. I have picked out the mistakes, habits, tricks and devices that are involved in order to show how these are the basis of ordinary practical thinking.

For instance, there are the four practical ways of being *right*.

R–1 Emotional rightness (currant cake effect)

R–2 Logical rightness (jig-saw puzzle effect)

R–3 Unique rightness (village Venus effect)

R–4 Recognition rightness (measles effect)

Unfortunately our culture has always insisted that being right is the end-result of flawless logic. This can be disastrous because as soon as someone has the *feeling* of being right he assumes that this must be based on absolute logic, which makes his conclusions impregnable and fit to be forced on others. In practice, being right is simply a *feeling* – almost an emotion. Logic is certainly one way to reach this feeling but, as is discussed in the book, there are other ways. The books also picks out the five major ways of being *wrong*:

M–1 Monorail mistake

M–2 Magnitude mistake

M–3 Misfit mistake

M–4 Must-be mistake

M–5 Miss-out mistake

These are the natural mistakes of the mind. Everyone makes them. You cannot avoid them. I make them all the time myself. But you can learn to recognize them even if only to smile or shrug as you watch them happen.

Understanding is the most important human thinking process: it enables the mind to make sense of the world around it. There are the five different ways to understand:

L–1 Simple description

L–2 Porridge words

L–3 Give it a name

L–4 The way it works

L–5 Full details

The code references (M–2, R–3, L–1, etc.) may seem rather artificial. The idea is that in time the different tricks of thinking may become so familiar that one can refer to them directly, for example 'That seems to be an M–2 there.' Giving them a name and a reference number means that one can focus on them and *talk* about them. It is rather like giving a new art style a name. Once the different tricks have become familiar then the code reference simply provides a convenient way of referring to them. It is *not* a matter of learning them so as to avoid them, but of learning them so as to recognize them as old friends.

The book also deals with the YES/NO system which is so basic to our traditional thinking. Although four major limitations are discussed, the system is acknowledged to be highly effective – provided that one keeps the dangers in mind. The book examines other aspects of thinking, including the two basic thinking processes; the two types of doubt; named-ideas and bundle-ideas; creativity; insight; humour; imagination; and the press-button idiom (probably the most important cultural change in thinking for centuries).

Parodoxes

Traditionally we have always supposed that it is the excellent logic of the human mind that is responsible for our wonderful thinking ability. In fact it seems to be not the logic of mind but its immense practicality that makes it so effective. Sometimes this practical aspect of thinking is directly contrary to the traditional idea of what thinking *should* be:

1. Some of our most useful thinking devices are really 'ignorance tools'. The 'black box' device allows us to make very good use of something while knowing very little about it.

2. Precise definition of terms has always been held up as the aim in thinking. And yet 'porridge words', which are deliberately vague and imprecise, are probably the most valuable thinking devices of all.

3. It may be that man is able to think so much better than animals only because he is more stupid. In thinking, the 'sharp brain' of animals which discriminates very quickly may be less useful than the 'blurry brain' of man which takes a long time to discriminate.

Philosophy and Thinking

A well-known professor some time ago described, at a public luncheon, how as a self-educating youngster he became interested in the process of thinking. He was told to go away and read Kant's

Critique of Pure Reason. He did so, but found that it had little to do with practical thinking. So he was told to go away again and read Russell and Whitehead's *Principia Mathematica*. But again he found that, though brilliant, it had little to do with practical thinking. He was kind enough to say that many years later he picked up one of my books and found that it did seem to be about practical thinking. It is hardly a matter of excellence or profundity but, as suggested earlier, if you happen to be in Italy a few mumbled words in Italian may be more appropriate than brilliant and fluent German.

The Thinking of Children

The three intellectual ages of man could be characterized as follows:

0–5 years..................the age of WHY

5–10 years..................the age of WHY NOT?

10–75+ years..................the age of BECAUSE

This opinion is partly based on the examination of hundreds of children's drawings obtained with the co-operation of *Where* (journal of the Advisory Centre for Education) and Sawston County Junior School. I used to believe that the creativity of children was simply the creativity of ignorance: that is to say that if you do not know how something is usually done you are more likely to come up with a fresh idea. But after various experiments I changed my mind, because even if you give a child in the 5–10-year age group something he knows very well (for example, a bicycle) he will still try to alter and improve it.

The Dog Exercising Machine is based on children's designs for a dog exercising machine. This design project was chosen because such machines do not already exist and so cannot be copied. Also, in addition to the mechanical aspect there is the aspect of psychology (dog-psychology) involved. There is an extraordinary range of designs, from robots and treadmills to exercise parks complete with tin-tack studded dog-mats so the dog cannot lie down and rest.

The book is about the way children think. But the thinking processes used by a child are no different to those used by an adult. But because the experience of a child is more limited, it becomes easier to separate the thinking process from the actual content. Thus the book provides a window through which one can look at the thinking process itself.

As a child reaches the age of 10–11 years, the BECAUSE intellectual age sets in very rapidly. This is the age of competence, of doing things as they should be done, of knowing all the reasons why things can only be done the way they have always been done. This is as it should be, because competence is always going to be more important than creativity. But it is not a matter of choosing between competence and creativity. One should have all the competence one needs – but with creativity alongside in order to make fuller use of that competence.

The huge importance of creativity in thinking can be seen when children are given a variety of difficult problems to solve. The book *Children Solve Problems* shows the creative way in which children approach adult problems. For instance, when children were asked to find a way of stopping a cat and a dog from fighting, their concepts went far beyond those traditionally used by politicians to stop racial and cultural conflicts.

I do not believe that there is any malicious intent on the part of the education system to stamp out the natural creativity of a child. There is simply no mechanism or effort to keep it alive. Whenever I have talked at university departments of education or at teachers' training colleges, I am always asked the same question: 'Creativity is all very well, but how do we judge whether a child's drawing is creative or not?' This is a sincere question. Teachers feel it is their duty to put ticks when something is right and crosses when something is wrong, in order to signpost the development of a child towards competent adulthood. But you cannot do this with creativity unless you have the experience and presumption of an art critic. So teachers restrict themselves to judging whether something has been done 'as it should be done'. That is easy to judge. The real answer to the question is that one must encourage the creative *process* but one does not need to judge the result: it is producing the idea that increases the creative skill of the child, not the judgment of that idea.

I have no quarrel with the competence function of education because the world needs competence, but I would like to see the creative WHY NOT attitude, which is so natural in the 5–10-year age group, maintained as a continuing strand alongside the competence function. That is why I wrote *Lateral Thinking: A Textbook of Creativity*: to provide, throughout education, a practical basis for one hour a week in which sheer creativity would get some encouragement.

Thinking as a Subject in Education

As suggested previously, creativity is only one aspect of thinking. I would like to see 'Thinking' taught as a subject in its own right, just as History or Geography or Science are now taught.

The Bertrand Russell quote used earlier claims that '... intelligence is a thing that can be fostered by known methods of education'. I do not agree with this at all – at least, in so far as thinking skill is a part of intelligence. Thinking as such is not taught in education. Everyone always assumes that it must be taught because that is what education is supposed to be all about. Traditional subjects are taught and taught very well, and it is supposed that in the course of learning these traditional subjects one's mind is being trained to think. I believe that this approach is inadequate.

First, I have done experiments on people who have had the very best education the world has to offer, and they themselves are the first to admit how little they know about thinking because they were never actually taught anything about it.

Second, even if the indirect rub-off method did work, it would be a ridiculously expensive and wasteful way of teaching thinking.

Some people claim that mathematics is the means of teaching thinking. This notion is not shared by mathematicians, who are fully conscious of the role of mathematics. If thinking were the same as mathematics, then the world would be a happy place because our mathematics are really very effective. Mathematics is a powerful tool of thinking, especially useful when one is working in a closed system, but it is not the whole of thinking or even the most applicable part for everyday affairs.

To be realistic, the chances of thinking being introduced into school curricula are slight. This is because education has become a self-justifying system whose only purpose is to perpetuate its own existence. Education sets the exams and satisfies itself by passing them. Subjects are taught for the very good reason that they were taught yesterday. Once again, it is not really a lack of vision on the part of the people in education because those I meet seem to have plenty of vision. But the system structure is more powerful than any dynamic individual: there are more victims than villains. Like any stable system, it tends to amplify the negative attitudes of those within it.

If education were a business which had to survive by maintaining its relevance to the external world it would doubtless be bankrupt within a few months, because so little money is spent on new product development. To maintain its market relevance it would have to spend 2–5 per cent of its budget on new product development (i.e., about £40–100 million). Of course, it is doing nothing of the sort. One only has to read the educational journals to find that educational effort is almost entirely concentrated on details of administration: controversies over class size, streaming versus unstreaming, tenure for headmasters, comprehensive versus grammar schools, free school meals, examinations, etc. It is the administrative and political structure of education which not unnaturally appeals most to politicians.

It is not a matter of increasing the strain on the already extended education budget by adding new subjects, but rather a matter of saving money by replacing obsolete subjects with simpler and more direct subjects like 'thinking'. For instance, it is said that the obsolete subject of Latin trains the mind, simply because no one can think of any other substantial justification for continuing to teach it. Fortunately Latin is so obsolete that it is almost gone, except in Oxford where academics justify its retention by that pathetic argument for continuity: can you prove it is doing any harm? At Imperial College in London only a third of those studying physics have any intention of being physicists. The rest are studying that expensive subject (expensive because of laboratory equipment, etc.) simply because at school physics was the only subject available which seemed to involve applied thinking.

The best argument against teaching 'thinking' as a subject is that there is no way of doing it. But I think it would be relatively easy to develop and test a full syllabus, and even though it seems unlikely to happen in this country, I still hope to set up an institute of Cognitive Research with this precise aim in mind. It is not something that will be brought about through individual inspiration, for it requires practical effort. But the education field does not think in terms of investment in new products as the technological field does. Consider the idea of 'cab-track', a futuristic and highly speculative scheme for having two-seater taxicabs on elevated rails. This is a speculative project which may not succeed commercially and even if it does succeed will involve heavy expenditure (and still only solve a very small part of the general city transport problem). Yet £25,000 are found for a feasibility study. This is followed some months later by a £250,000 government contract for further research. If only education had that sort of new project outlook. It is a pity it does not, because the subject of 'thinking' is possibly more important than a futuristic taxicab system. The simple difference is that people in education are largely administrators who are terrified that a new product might prove too successful and so saddle them with the burden of having to do something about it. The only possible reason for change is fear of obsolescence, and since education is a self-justifying system there can never be any such fear.

The danger of thinking

Quite recently the headmaster of a school told me that he agreed in principle with the teaching of thinking but he asked whether in practice it would not simply make people discontented and dissatisfied. Since most pupils (from this school) were going to spend their lives at factory benches, it was safer to teach them just enough to do that properly. I do not think that the headmaster actually believed this himself; he was passing on to me views that had been expressed to him by others, perhaps other headmasters, perhaps his staff, in order to see how the question might be answered. Or it may be that this point of view is far more widespread in education than I suppose.

The Flight from Reason

We are supposed to be living in an anti-intellectual age. There is supposed to be a flight from reason towards emotional and sexual hedonism; towards mysticism, drugs and dreams; towards putting the responsibility for life on to the stars, Freudian traumas or our animal natures. This flight is perhaps more exaggerated in America than it is here.

But it is not a flight from reason. It is a flight from the sterility and futility of the old idiom of thinking that still completely dominates our intellectual establishments. It is a flight from the click-clack of well-educated minds as they proceed with their old-fashioned concept-knitting, making garments that serve only to keep their wearer smug and warm. It is the flight of those who consider All Souls College at Oxford an enclave of intellectual fiddlers.

In my own experience I have found, especially among young people, not an anti-intellectualism but on the contrary a huge yearning for new idioms of thinking – a yearning that most people, especially in education, have not noticed. At a recent talk to a student society, instead of the expected audience of forty to fifty usual on such occasions, over three hundred turned up. This has happened again and again. I have been invited to speak at three-quarters of the universities in England and have managed to speak at well over half. On one occasion I was asked by four different departments in the same university to speak on suggested dates all within the same month. There has been just as much interest from polytechnics and art colleges.

Since those inviting me to speak have not usually read my books and have only the vaguest idea of what I am going to talk about, the invitation (at least on the first occasion) suggests more their own yearning for a new idiom of thinking than interest or acceptance of my ideas. It has been interesting to note in what fields this open-minded attitude of exploration has shown itself. There are some strange bedfellows among those interested – from the Irish Government Treasury Department to hippies in New York; from the four largest corporations in Europe to the leading art colleges and major conferences on art education; from IBM, Univac, etc., to primary schools; from engineering companies to the three largest advertising agencies in the world; from child welfare officers to New York city administrators.

Over-all, there has been interest from artists, architects, designers, engineers, teachers, computer scientists, hippies, system analysts, operations research scientists, big business corporations, ecologists, mathematicians and physicists. This is not to say that these groups have liked my ideas or found anything useful in them, but simply that they have been eager to look and find out. The alignment is perhaps not so strange when one considers that all these different groups have one thing in common: the need for new ideas. The obvious gaps in the list relate to those fields which are not at all interested in changing ideas. For instance politicians, who – no matter how revolutionary – are interested only in insisting that their rigid idea is better than your rigid idea. Philosophers also have an interest in preserving the rigidity of those concepts and modes of thought that are their platform. Some countries are more interested in changing ideas than others. For instance, more hardcover copies of my first book on lateral thinking were sold per head of the population in Japan than were sold of *Love Story* in America (supposed to be the best-selling novel of all time). But even in England, which is traditionally wary of new ideas, there seems to be growing interest – to the extent that there were

50 per cent more people at the *Observer* seminar on lateral thinking than there were at the one on consumerism given by Ralph Nader.

The New Word PO

I hesitated before introducing the idea of the new word PO. The outraged reactions to the idea in England (but not in America, Germany, Holland or Japan) showed that the hesitation was justified. But I feel that it is better to try and survive this outrage than draw back from PO. In any case the outrage is partly based on nursery trauma.

Just as NO is the basic operational tool for logical thinking, so PO is the basic operational tool for lateral thinking. The word NO crystallizes the function of logic, which is to reject ideas that do not fit. The word PO crystallizes the function of lateral thinking, which is to move from one way of looking at things to another. NO is the tool of judgment: PO is the tool of creative exploration. Language and thought tend to preserve established patterns: that is why we need a device like PO which enables us to use ideas in new ways in order to break out of such patterns. PO is a crystallization of the whole area of creativity, open-endedness, alternative perceptions, restructuring, insight, humour, exploration and discontinuity. At first PO seems strange, artificial and unnecessary even to those who see the need for lateral thinking. But when they have got more used to the idea, such people usually see the need for some crystallization of the whole concept of lateral thinking into a usable symbol for language and thought. PO is used both to generate new ideas and to challenge the rigid dogmatism of fixed ways of looking at things.

Be Obscure

I used to believe that if you had something to say you ought to try and say it as simply as possible even if you did not succeed. I now feel that this might be a mistaken or even presumptuous attitude. Consider the following advantages of writing in a complex fashion:

1. If the writing is sufficiently obscure, a high-priest cult develops to

explain you to the world – and usually makes an excellent job of it. The high-priests do rather better than one can do oneself. They have a real sense of commitment and contribution in their job of interpretation. The more complex and obscure the writing, the higher the contribution of the high-priests and the greater their sense of fulfilment.

2. If the writing is sufficiently obscure then individual readers can interpret it in individual ways. Each one can find in it support for his own views even though these may differ widely from one person to another.

3. Obscure writing gives rise to different interpretations, and that means controversy and discussion. Since so many of the best brains are trained to function only in a critical fashion, the opportunity for controversy is eagerly welcomed. With something that is written simply, you either see the point or you do not.

4. If the writing is sufficiently obscure, then no reader can pretend that he knows it all already because he must always be afraid that in the obscurity lies something that he has not yet discovered.

In contrast to these real advantages of writing in an obscure fashion, there are few advantages in writing simply, apart from personal satisfaction. Moreover there is one very serious disadvantage in writing simply: you can never make someone see *beyond the limits of his vision.* A person of limited vision reads something that has been written simply, and, because he *can* understand it, is convinced that there is nothing more to it than is contained within that limited vision. If it was obscure and he could not understand it, the natural supposition would be that there was something more profound than he could grasp.

Stimulation

In art a picture must have ambiguity and complexity in order to be interesting. A picture that has neither is more like a road sign than a picture. This is another reason why complexity and ambiguity in writing may well be better than simplicity. After all, a road sign is completely uninteresting if you do not happen to be going that way. On the other hand, if you have been looking for a particular direction indicator then the road sign is more valuable than any picture.

In my writing I do not want to set down dogma, creed or instruction but to stimulate the reader to look in different directions. If his vision is limited then he will see nothing in those directions – and will be fully justified in saying so. If his vision is good he will see more than there is to see – more even than I can see myself. Once you set out to stimulate rather than instruct, you place yourself at the mercy of those you are trying to stimulate. If there is much to stimulate they might appreciate the value of the stimulation. If there is nothing to stimulate then the stimulation attempt is a true waste of their time.

In practice there is no reason whatsoever why a person should be persuaded to believe that there is more to be seen than he himself can see. There is nothing at all wrong with limited vision. As with logic, the danger lies only in the arrogance that attends limited vision: 'If I cannot see more, then there can be nothing more.'

Presentation

Although I do have genuine doubts about the wisdom of trying to write simply, I do not have any doubts at all about the visual layout of books. I hate fusty, badly designed books. One reviewer (in *The Economist*) commented that one of my books was very well presented and packaged, and then went on to suggest that somehow this made him suspicious because advertising was also well presented and packaged. I refuse to accept that poor design is a necessary part of the 'seriousness' of something.

Summary of the Books

The Five-Day Course in Thinking (Allen Lane the Penguin Press, London, 1968; Penguin, Harmondsworth, 1969)
Simple problems (involving knives, bottles, matchboxes and the L-game) are used as *opportunities* for the reader to watch his own mind in action. Specific comments on the thinking process are given as suggestions for the sort of comments he might make himself as he comes across the weaknesses and strengths in his own thinking. This matters much more than actually solving the problems, which would increase the reader's ego rather than his experience. There are in fact three five-day courses: insight thinking, sequential thinking and strategic thinking.

The Use of Lateral Thinking (Jonathan Cape, London, 1967. U.S. title: *New Think*)
The *basic* introduction to lateral thinking. A short book which shows how lateral thinking differs from the traditional logical sequential thinking (vertical thinking). The book outlines the principles of lateral thinking and explains why it is needed for creativity. It is strongly suggested that anyone interested in lateral thinking should start with this book before going on to more specialized books.

The Mechanism of Mind (Jonathan Cape, London, 1969)
The most fundamental of all the books, because it shows how my ideas about thinking arise directly from consideration of the physical structure of mind as a particular type of information system. The first half deals with the system basis of mind and shows how phenomena which are usually considered to be mysterious are in fact the ordinary behaviour of an organization of nerve cells. The explanation is given without jargon and in easy stages, by means of such simple models as a dish of table jelly. The second half of the book shows why this type of mind must have certain *inevitable* faults which show up in our thinking. Such processes as polarization, concept rigidity, sequential and insight learning, humour, logic, unity of attention and limited attention are explained. There is also a practical suggestion for overcoming, in particular, the difficulty of escaping from fixed patterns.

The book deals with mind in a direct physical way which is quite different from the traditional philosophic word playground of philosophy. It is of particular use to those who do not want to accept ideas simply because 'they sound right' but want to know what is behind them.

Lateral Thinking: A Textbook of Creativity (Ward Lock Educational, London, 1970)
A practical book written for schools. The various techniques of lateral thinking are described in detail, and problems and exercises for practising the techniques are also given. The book is intended as a basis for teaching creativity throughout education (perhaps for one hour a week). It is of direct use to individuals involved in the generation of new ideas (designers, for example), and may also be used by parents who feel that it might be a long time before formal education includes the teaching of creativity.

Lateral Thinking For Management (McGraw-Hill, London, and the American Management Association, New York, 1971)
The idea ingredient in management is getting more important all the time. To cope with rapidly changing circumstances you must be able to escape from outworn ideas, and to cope with increasing market competition you must be able to generate effective new ideas. For management, creativity is not a philosophical discussion but a needed tool. This book treats creativity not as a magic gift but as a skill which can be developed as part of management equipment. Everyone who has to think needs some creativity to supplement logical processing. Those whose special task it is to generate ideas (senior executives, planners, research and marketing executives, problem-solvers, advertisers, etc.) need to develop an especial degree of creativity. The book explains the basic principles of lateral thinking and gives specific techniques for applying them both on an individual and a group basis. The management of creativity within an organization is described – and also the dangers of creativity. The four main areas demanding creativity are: innovation, problem-solving, simplification, and alternatives for decision and planning.

The Dog Exercising Machine (Jonathan Cape, London, 1970)
A book on how children think. Designs by children aged 4–14 for a dog exercising machine. Comments on each design, and also general points on children's thinking, which provide an uncluttered window through which to look at the thinking of adults. The 5–10-year period (the age of WHY NOT?) is probably the most creative one of our lives. Why do we grow out of it?

Children Solve Problems (Allen Lane the Penguin Press, and Penguin Education, 1972)
A number of different problems were given to children to solve: how to stop a cat and a dog from fighting; how to weigh an elephant; design a fun machine; how to deal with badmen; invent a sleep machine; how to speed up the building of a house; furnish a space rocket, etc. The problems were deliberately chosen to illustrate different aspects of problem-solving (political, moral, mechanical, organizational, system behaviour, etc.). In the previous book on children's creativity the emphasis was on the basic characteristics of children's thinking. In this book the emphasis is on the way the different types of problem are handled. It seems that adults have much to learn from the problem-solving ability of children. Children start out as fluent thinkers. The need to at least preserve this fluency during the course of education is discussed.

Practical Thinking (Jonathan Cape, London, 1971)
This book is *not* about lateral thinking; it is about practical everyday thinking, and is based on an experimental investigation into the thinking process. The natural habits, tricks, tools and devices of ordinary thinking are put on the table for all to see. There are the four different ways of being right (logical is only one of them), the five ways of being wrong, and also the five basic levels of understanding. After reading the book you should be able to pick out these patterns both in your own thinking and in the thinking of others. The book explains how much of the effectiveness of the mind arises from its use of *practical* 'ignorance tools' like 'black boxes' and 'porridge words'. It discusses the arrogance and righteousness of the YES/NO system, and it suggests the importance of humour in thinking.

It also explains why man may be able to think better than animals simply because he is more stupid than them. The book turns upside down many of our traditional views of thinking, but above all it makes it possible to treat thinking as a *practical* process. It makes it possible to talk about thinking and the tricks involved. A new approach to thinking, 'Think–2', is suggested for dealing with conflict situations: not by argument, but by a perceptual mapping of the starting positions.

Technology Today (Routledge & Kegan Paul, London, 1971)
A collection of five pieces by different contributors writing about the present and future place of technology in society: 'For society to quarrel with technology is like a man quarrelling with his legs.' It suggests new attitudes that are needed in the control of technology.

Beyond Yes and No To PO (Simon and Schuster, New York, 1972)
This book looks directly at the YES/NO system which has always been the basis of our particular culture's way of thinking. The YES/NO system is seen to be based on selection by rejection; on judgment by reference to fixed absolutes; on definitions, classifications, categories; on polarizations and the security of knowing who is right and who is wrong; on the changing of ideas by the conflict method. This way of thinking is responsible for our development as an effective civilization, but it is also responsible for most of our troubles both in the past and in the present.

The truth is that we have never developed any method for changing ideas except conflict. Today we need more than ever to change our ideas in order to cope with rapidly altering circumstances, and yet the conflict method is too bloody to be workable any longer. To counter the arrogant certainty of the YES/NO system and to provide a means for creative change we may have to introduce PO as a basic element into our culture, on an equal status with YES and NO. YES is the basis of the belief system; NO is the basis of the logical system; PO is the basis of the creative system. YES confirms patterns; NO preserves them; and PO creates new ones.